TODAY'S F[...] ROCK HITS
FOR UKULELE

ISBN 978-1-4950-1698-1

HAL•LEONARD®
CORPORATION
7777 W. BLUEMOUND RD. P.O. BOX 13819 MILWAUKEE, WI 53213

For all works contained herein:
Unauthorized copying, arranging, adapting, recording, Internet posting, public performance,
or other distribution of the printed music in this publication is an infringement of copyright.
Infringers are liable under the law.

Visit Hal Leonard Online at
www.halleonard.com

Dirty Paws

Words and Music by Of Monsters And Men

Copyright © 2012 Sony/ATV Music Publishing LLC, Is Your Mother Home, NannaBH Music and Mussi Music
All Rights Administered by Sony/ATV Music Publishing LLC, 424 Church Street, Suite 1200, Nashville, TN 37219
International Copyright Secured   All Rights Reserved

Additional Lyrics

2. Her dirty paws and furry coat,
   She ran down the forest slope.
   The forest of talking trees,
   They used to sing about the birds and the bees.
   The bees had declared a war;
   The sky wasn't big enough for them all.
   The birds, they got help from below,
   From dirty paws and the creatures of snow.

3. So, for a while, things were cold.
   They were scared down in their holes.
   The forest that once was green
   Was colored black by those killing machines.
   But she and her furry friends
   Took down the queen bee and her men.
   And that's how the story goes,
   The story of the beast with those four dirty paws.

5 Years Time

By Charlie Fink

First note

Verse
Moderately bright

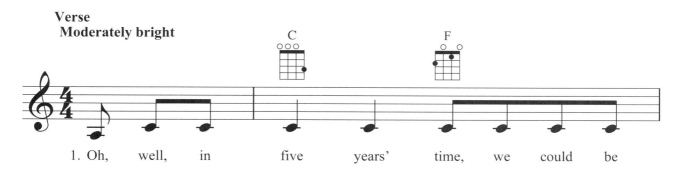

1. Oh, well, in five years' time, we could be

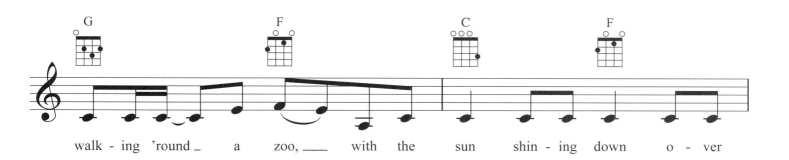

walk - ing 'round _ a zoo, ___ with the sun shin - ing down o - ver

me and you. And there'll be love in the bod - ies of the

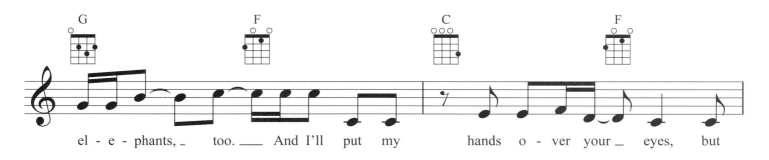

el - e - phants, _ too. ___ And I'll put my hands o - ver your _ eyes, but

Copyright © 2008 HANGMAN MUSIC LTD.
All Rights in the U.S. and Canada Controlled and Administered by UNIVERSAL - POLYGRAM INTERNATIONAL PUBLISHING, INC.
All Rights Reserved   Used by Permission

_____ to smoke _ all those stu - pid lit - tle cig - a - rettes and

drink stu - pid wine, _ 'cause it's what we need-ed to have a good time. _ But it was

Chorus

fun, fun, fun when we were drink - ing. It was fun, fun, fun

when we were drunk. _ And it _____ was fun, fun, fun _____

when we were laugh - ing. It was fun, fun, fun, _____

Interlude

oh, it was fun. _

7

all through our minds. _ And it - 'll be love, love, love ___

all o - ver her ___ face, and love, love, love ___

Verse

all o - ver mine. _ 4. And though, ad - mit -'ly, all these mo - ments are just ___

___ in my ___ head, _ I'll be think-ing 'bout ___ them ___ as I'm ly -

ing in bed. ___ And I know ___ that, ad - mit - 'ly, it might not

e - ven come ___ true, ___ but in my mind, I'm ___ hav - ing a pret - ty good

Outro-Chorus

1st time only: Whistle continues

Oh, there'll be love, love, love

wher - ev - er you go. There'll be love, love, love

wher - ev - er you go. There'll be love, love, love _____

Whistle ends

wher - ev - er you go. There'll be love, love, love ___

wher - ev - er you go. There'll be love.

Gone Gone Gone

Words and Music by Gregg Wattenberg, Derek Fuhrmann and Todd Clark

1. When life leaves _ you high and dry, I'll be at __ your door to-night if

you need _ help, ___ if you need _ help. ___ I'll

shut down _ the cit - y lights; I'll lie, cheat, _ I'll beg and bribe to

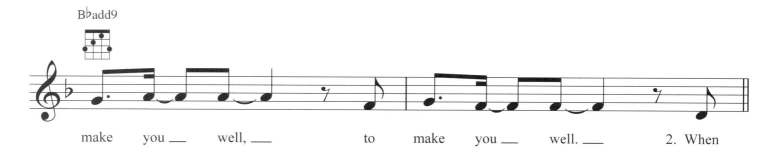

make you __ well, ___ to make you __ well. ___ 2. When

© 2012 EMI APRIL MUSIC INC., G WATT MUSIC, EGG SONGS PUBLISHING and AE FUHRMANN PUBLISHING
All Rights for G WATT MUSIC Controlled and Administered by EMI APRIL MUSIC INC.
All Rights Reserved   International Copyright Secured   Used by Permission

Verse

en - e - mies __ are at your door, I'll car - ry you __ a - way __ from war if
(3.) fall __ like __ a sta - tue, I'm gon' be __ there ____ to catch you, put you

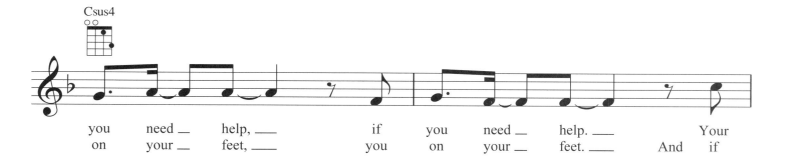

you need __ help, ___ if you need __ help. ___ Your
on your __ feet, ___ you on your __ help. ___ And if

hope dan - gling by a string, I'll share in ___ your suf - fer - ing __ to
your well __ is emp - ty, not a thing will __ pre - vent me. __ Tell me

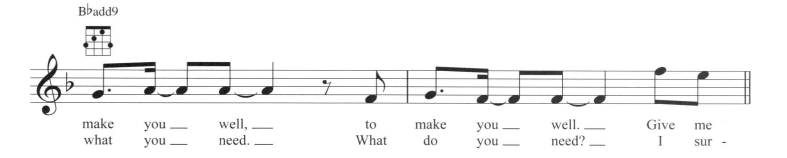

make you ___ well, ___ to make you __ well. ___ Give me
what you __ need. ___ What do you __ need? ___ I sur -

Pre-Chorus

rea - sons to be - lieve _____ that you would do the same for me.
ren - der hon - est - ly; _____ you've al - ways done the same for me.

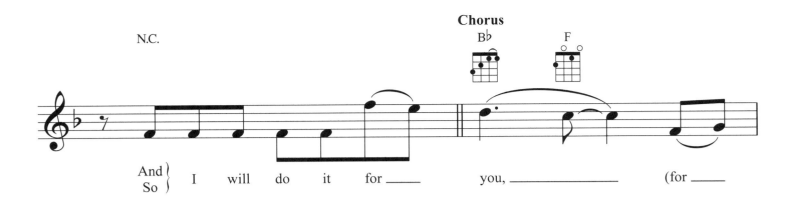

And / So } I will do it for ____ you, _____ (for ____

you.) _____ Ba - by, I'm ____ not mov - ing on, ____ I'll love you long _____

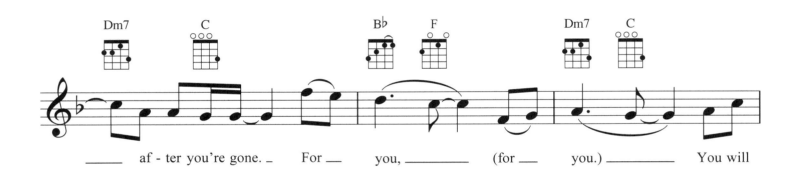

____ af - ter you're gone. __ For ____ you, _____ (for ____ you.) _____ You will

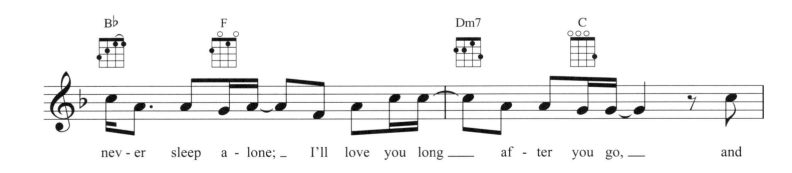

nev - er sleep a - lone; __ I'll love you long _____ af - ter you go, ___ and

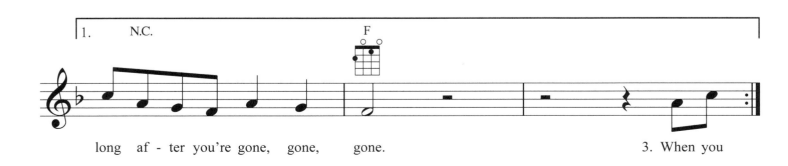

long af - ter you're gone, gone, gone.   3. When you

14

Bridge

long af - ter you're gone, gone, gone. You're my back - bone, ___ you're my cor - ner - stone, ___

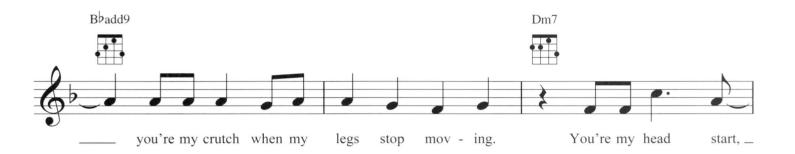

___ you're my crutch when my legs stop mov - ing. You're my head start, ___

___ you're my rug - ged ___ heart, ___ you're the pulse that I've al - ways need - ed.

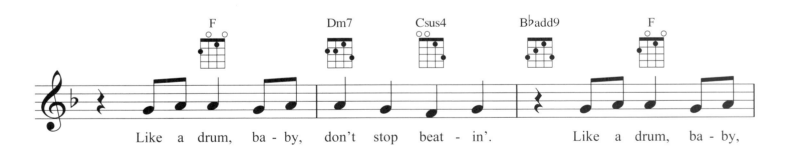

Like a drum, ba - by, don't stop beat - in'. Like a drum, ba - by,

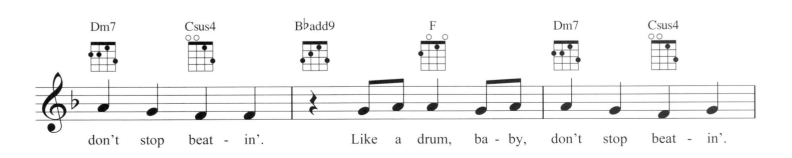

don't stop beat - in'. Like a drum, ba - by, don't stop beat - in'.

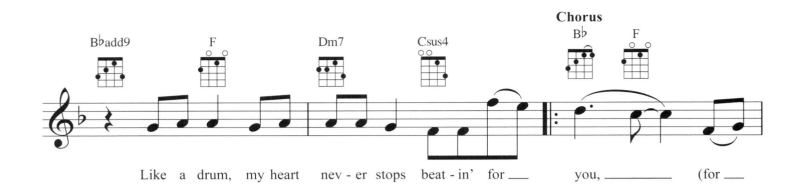

Like a drum, my heart nev - er stops beat - in' for ___ you, _____ (for ___

you.) _____ Ba - by, I'm ___ not mov - ing on. ___ I'll love you long ___

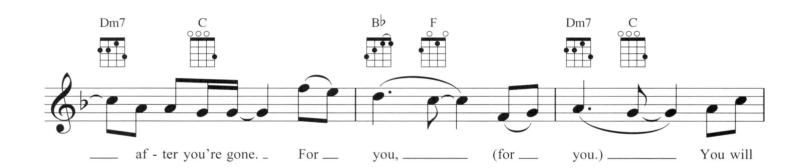

___ af - ter you're gone. _ For ___ you, _____ (for ___ you.) _____ You will

nev - er sleep a - lone; _ I'll love you long ___ af - ter you go. ___ For ___

nev - er sleep a - lone; _ I'll love you long, ___ long ___ af - ter you go. _

Outro

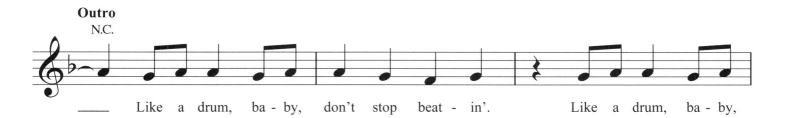

_____ Like a drum, ba - by, don't stop beat - in'. Like a drum, ba - by,

don't stop beat - in'. Like a drum, ba - by, don't stop beat - in'.

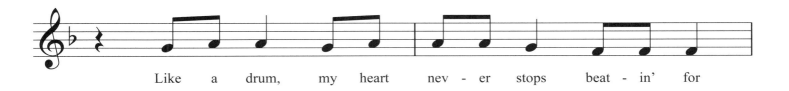

Like a drum, my heart nev - er stops beat - in' for

you. And long af - ter you're gone, gone,

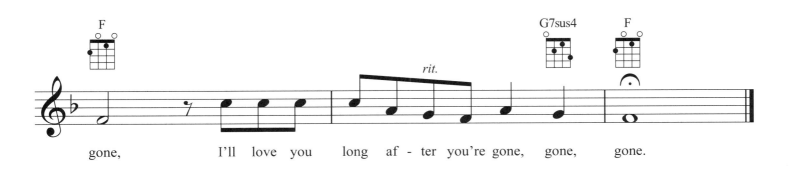

gone, I'll love you long af - ter you're gone, gone, gone.

Helplessness Blues

Words and Music by Robin Pecknold

1. I was raised up be-liev-ing I was some-how u-
(2., 3.) *See additional lyrics*

nique, like a snow - flake, dis - tinct a-mong snow-flakes, u -

nique in each way you can see. And now, af - ter some

think - ing, I'd say I'd rath - er be a

func - tion - ing cog in some great ma - chin - er - y, serv - ing some-thing be-yond

Copyright © 2011 Foxes Fellowship
All Rights Administered by Kobalt Songs Music Publishing
All Rights Reserved   Used by Permission

Gold

Bridge

hair in the sun - light, _____ oh, _____

my light in the dawn. _____ oh, oh, _____ oh,

If I _____ had an or -
_____ oh, _____ oh, oh, _____

- chard, I'd work 'til I'm _____ sore.
_____ oh, _____ oh, _____ oh.

1.

If I _____ had an or - chard, I'd work 'til I'm _____

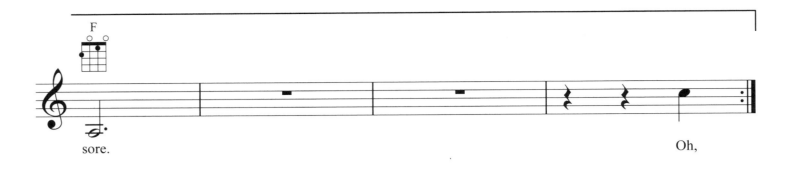

sore.   Oh,

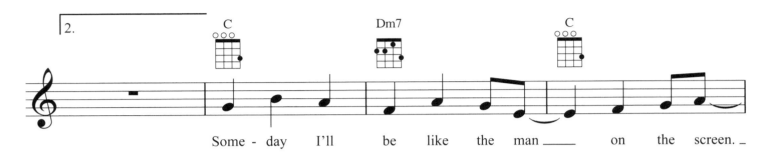

Some - day   I'll   be   like   the   man _____   on   the   screen. _

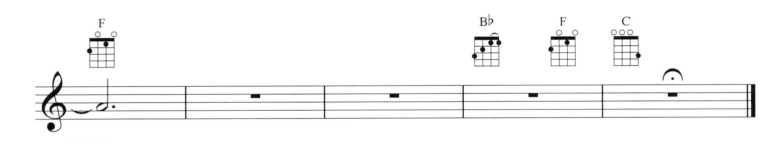

Additional Lyrics

2. What's my name? What's my station?
   Oh, just tell me what I should do.
   I don't need to be kind to the armies of night
   That will do such injustice to you,
   Or bow down and be grateful
   And say, "Sure, take all that you see"
   To the men who move only in dimly-lit halls
   And determine my future for me.

Chorus: And I don't, I don't know who to believe.
   I'll get back to you someday soon; you will see.

3. If I know only one thing,
   It's that everything that I see
   Of the world outside is so inconceivable,
   Often I barely can speak.
   Yeah, I'm tongue-tied and dizzy,
   And I can't keep it to myself.
   What good is it to sing helplessness blues?
   Why should I wait for anyone else?

Chorus: And I know, I know you will keep me on the shelf.
   I'll come back to you someday soon myself.

Ho Hey

Words and Music by Jeremy Fraites and Wesley Schultz

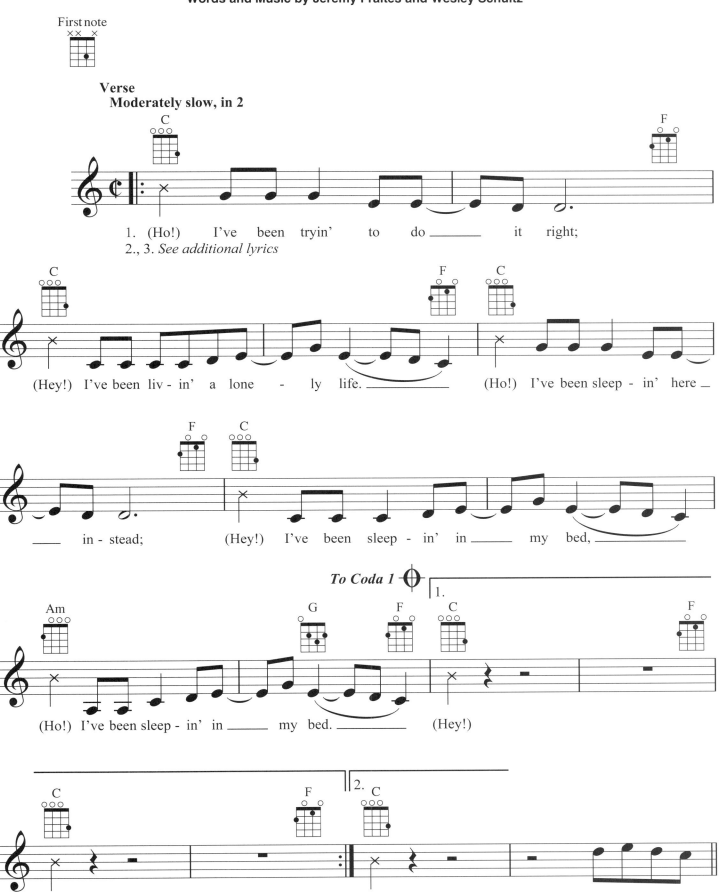

Copyright © 2011 The Lumineers
All Rights Exclusively Administered by Songs Of Kobalt Music Publishing
All Rights Reserved   Used by Permission

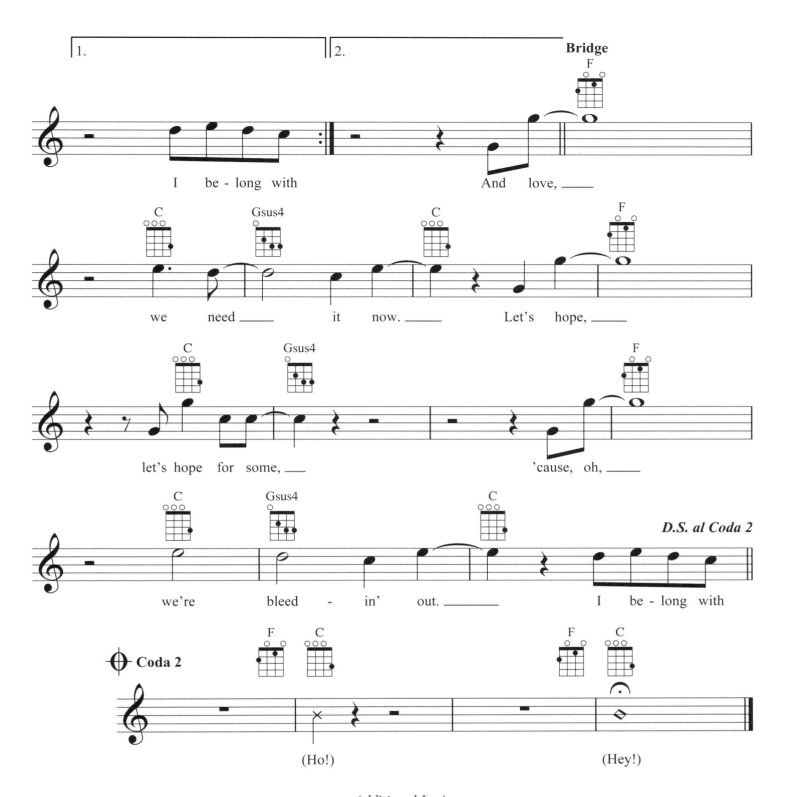

Additional Lyrics

2. (Ho!) So show me, family,
   (Hey!) All the blood that I will bleed.
   (Ho!) I don't know where I belong,
   (Hey!) I don't know where I went wrong,
   (Ho!) But I can write a song.
   (Hey!)

3. (Ho!) I don't think you're right for him.
   (Hey!) Look at what it might have been if you
   (Ho!) Took a bus to Chinatown.
   (Hey!) I'd be standing on Canal
   (Ho!) And Bowery. *(To Coda 1)*

Home

Words and Music by Jade Castrinos and Alex Ebert

(Whistle)

Girl: 1. Al - a - bam - a,   Ar - kan - sas,
Guy: 2. I'll   fol - low you in - to   the park,

I   do   love   my   ma   and   pa,   not   the   way ___   that   I   do ___   love ___
through   the   jun - gle, through   the   dark.   Girl, I've   nev - er   loved   one ___   like ___

Copyright © 2009 BMG Monarch, Caravan Touchdown, BMG Blue and Jadey Rae
All Rights Administered by BMG Rights Management (US) LLC
All Rights Reserved   Used by Permission

_____ you. _____   *Guy:* Well, ho - ly mo - ley, me oh my, __
_____ you. _____   *Girl:* Moats and boats and wa - ter - falls, _

you're the ap - ple of my eye. __   Girl, I've nev - er loved one __ like __
al - ley - ways and pay-phone calls. _   I've been __ ev - 'ry-where with __

_____ you. _____   *Girl:* Man oh man, you're my best friend, I
_____ you. _____   *Guy:* Laugh un - til we think we'll die,

scream it to __ the noth-ing - ness. __   There ain't noth - ing that __ I
bare-foot on __ a sum-mer night, _   nev - er could be sweet - er than _ with

need. _____   *Guy:* Well, hot and heav - y, pump - kin pie,
you. _____   *Girl:* And in the streets you're run - ning free,

choc -'late can - dy, Je - sus Christ, there ain't noth - in' please me more _ than
like it's on - ly you and me. Jeez, _____ you're some - thin' _ to

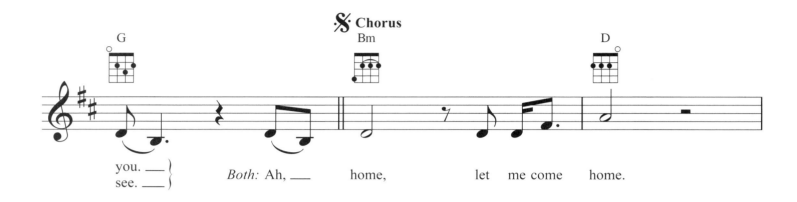

𝄋 **Chorus**

you. ___ }
see. ___ }   *Both:* Ah, ___ home, let me come home.

Home is ___ wher-ev - er I'm with you. ___ Ah, ___ home, let me come

To Coda ⊕

home. _____ (1., 2.) Home is ___ wher-ev - er I'm with you. ___
(D.S.) Home is ___ when I'm a - lone with you. ___

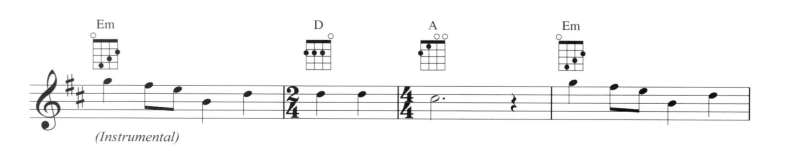

(Instrumental)

28

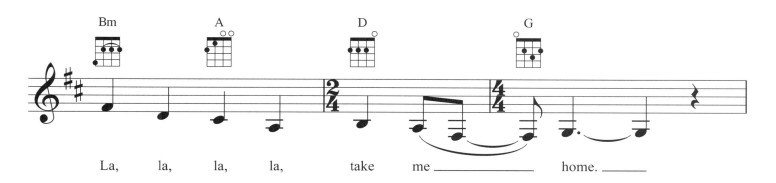

La, la, la, la, take me _____ home. _____

1. A7   N.C.

Guy:

Girl:

Ma - ma, I'm ___ com - in' home. ___   *(Instrumental)*

2. A7   *D.S. al Coda*

Ma - ma, I'm ___ com - in' home. ___   Ah, ___

Outro
Coda Bm   D

Al - a - bam - a, Ar - kan - sas, _____

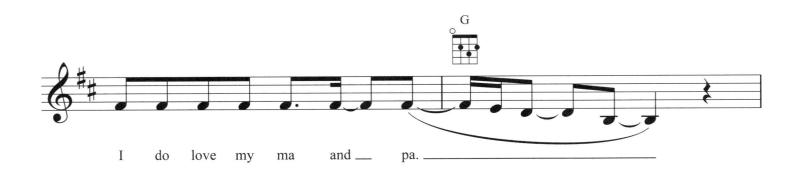

I do love my ma and ___ pa. _____

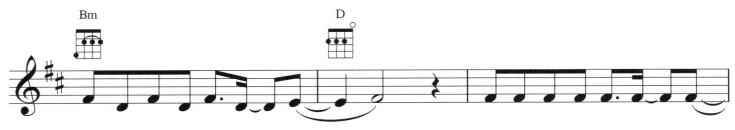

Moats and boats and wa - ter - falls, _____ al - ley-ways and pay - phone _ calls. _

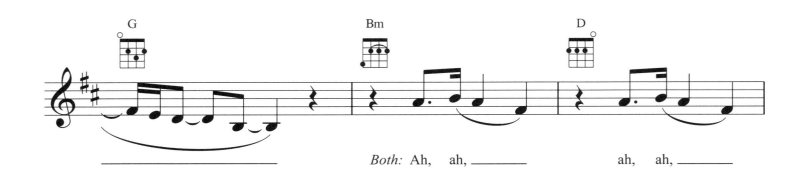

_____ *Both:* Ah, ah, _____ ah, ah, _____

home is ___ when I'm a - lone with you. Ah, ah, _____

ah, ah, _____ home is ___ when I'm a - lone with you. ___

Little Talks

Words and Music by Of Monsters And Men

Copyright © 2012 Sony/ATV Music Publishing LLC, NannaBH Music and Mussi Music
All Rights Administered by Sony/ATV Music Publishing LLC, 424 Church Street, Suite 1200, Nashville, TN 37219
International Copyright Secured   All Rights Reserved

Pre-Chorus

Both: 'Cause though the truth may var - y, this ___

ship ___ will car - ry our ___ bod - ies

safe to ___ shore. *(Instrumental)* *Hey!* Don't

Chorus

(1., 3., 4.) lis - ten to a word I ___ say. *Hey!* The
(2.) *Instrumental*

screams all sound the ___ same. *Hey!* And though the

truth may var - y, this ___ ship ___ will

33

I and Love and You

Words and Music by Scott Avett, Seth Avett and Robert Crawford

1. Load the car __ and write the note. __

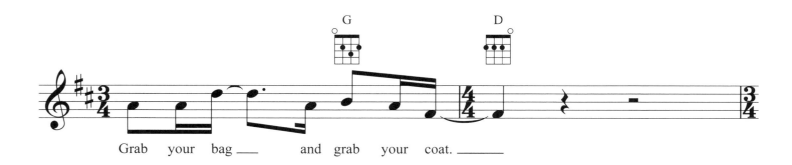

Grab your bag __ and grab your coat. _____

Tell the ones _ that need to know: _____ we are head-ed north.

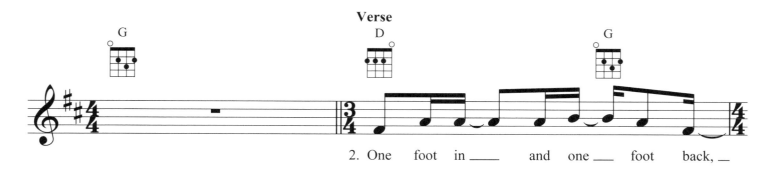

2. One foot in ____ and one __ foot back, __

Copyright © 2009 First Big Snow Publishing, Ramseur Family Fold Music, Nemoivmusic and Truth Comes True Publishing
All Rights Administered by BMG Rights Management (US) LLC
All Rights Reserved   Used by Permission

but it don't pay ___ to live like

that. So I cut the ties ___ and I jumped the tracks, ___

___ for nev-er to ___ re-turn. ___ Ah,

𝄋 **Chorus**

Brook - lyn, Brook - lyn, take me in. ___ Are

you a-ware ___ the shape I'm in? ___ My

hands, they shake; ___ my head, it spins. ___ Ah, ___

day; _____ look at the things _ I _____

Chorus

_____ do. Ah, Brook - lyn, Brook - lyn, take me in. __

__ Are you a - ware _ the shape I'm in? _

____ My hands, they shake; my head, it spins. _

____ Ah, _ Brook - lyn, Brook - lyn, take me in. _

1.

2. **Verse**

____ ____ 6. Dumbed down and numbed _ by time and age, _

I Bet My Life

Words and Music by Daniel Reynolds, Daniel Sermon,
Benjamin McKee and Daniel Platzman

Copyright © 2014 SONGS OF UNIVERSAL, INC., IMAGINE DRAGONS PUBLISHING and SONGS FOR KIDINAKORNER
All Rights Controlled and Administered by SONGS OF UNIVERSAL, INC.
All Rights Reserved   Used by Permission

Pre-Chorus

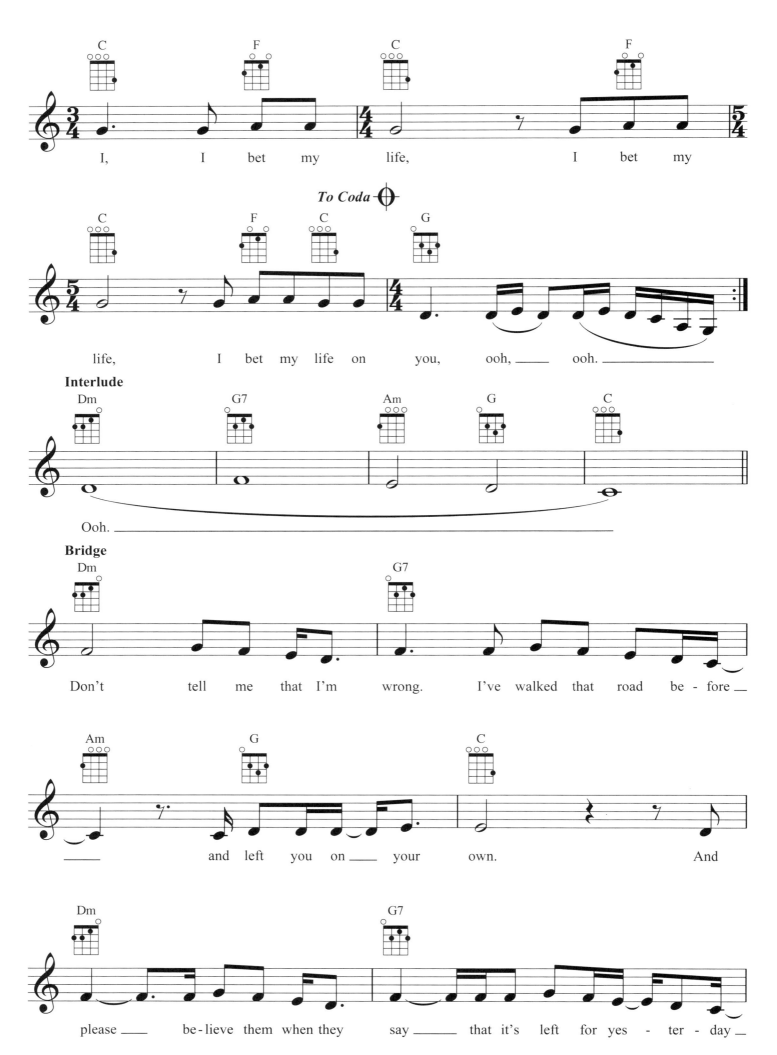

I, I bet my life, I bet my

To Coda ⊕

life, I bet my life on you, ooh, ____ ooh. ____

Interlude

Ooh. ____

Bridge

Don't tell me that I'm wrong. I've walked that road be - fore ____

____ and left you on ____ your own. And

please ____ be-lieve them when they say ____ that it's left for yes - ter - day ____

and the rec-ords that ___ I play. ___ Please for-give ___

___ me for all _____ I've done. So

Outro

you, ooh, _____ ooh. _____ I, I

bet my, I bet my, I bet my…

I, I bet my life, _____ I

bet my life, _____ I bet my… *(Instrumental)*

I Will Wait

Words and Music by Mumford & Sons

Copyright © 2012 UNIVERSAL MUSIC PUBLISHING LTD.
All Rights in the U.S. and Canada Controlled and Administered by UNIVERSAL - POLYGRAM INTERNATIONAL TUNES, INC.
All Rights Reserved   Used by Permission

Interlude

Bridge

Raise _____ my _____ hands, _____
bow _____ my _____ head, _____

paint my spir - it gold. _____ And
keep my heart _____

_____ slow. _____

Outro-Chorus

_____ 'Cause I will _ wait, I will _ wait for you.

And I will _ wait, I will _ wait for you.

And

Little Lion Man

Words and Music by Mumford & Sons

1. Weep for your-self, my man. You'll nev - er be what is in your
2. Trem-ble for your-self, my man. You know that you have seen this all be -

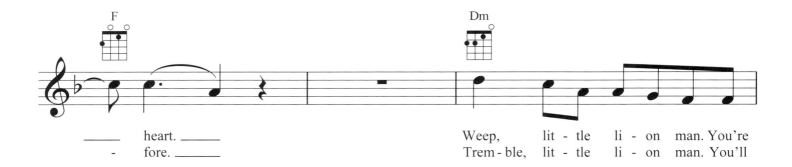

____ heart. ____
 - fore. ____

Weep, lit - tle li - on man. You're
Trem - ble, lit - tle li - on man. You'll

not as brave as you were at the ____ start. ____
nev - er set - tle an - y of your ____ scores. ____

Your

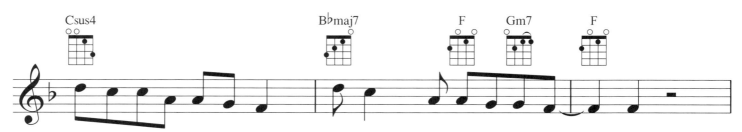

Rate your-self and rake your-self, take all the cour-age you have ____ left,
grace is wast-ed in your face, your bold-ness stands a - lone a - mong the wreck.

Copyright © 2009 UNIVERSAL MUSIC PUBLISHING LTD.
All Rights in the U.S. and Canada Controlled and Administered by UNIVERSAL - POLYGRAM INTERNATIONAL TUNES, INC.
All Rights Reserved   Used by Permission

and waste it on   fix - ing all the   prob - lems that you made in your own __
Now, learn   from your moth - er, or else   spend your days   bit - ing your own __

Chorus

__ head. }
__ neck. }

But it was   not your fault, but mine. __

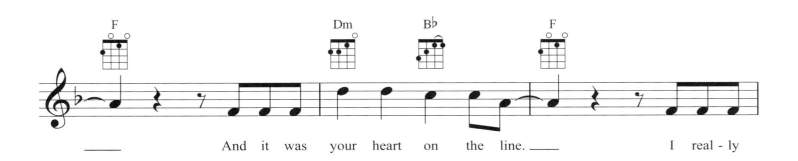

__   And it was   your heart on the line. ____   I real - ly

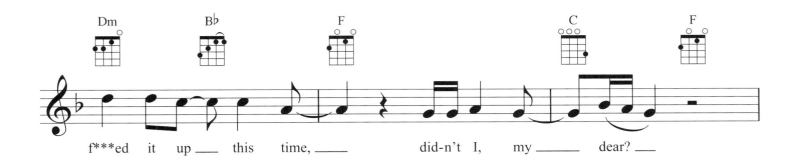

f***ed it up __ this   time, ____   did - n't I, my ____ dear? ____

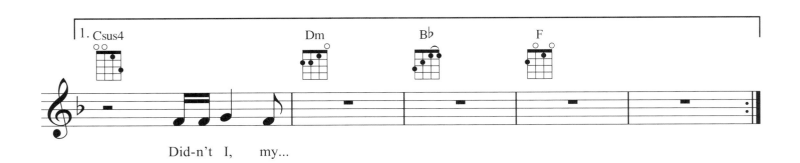

Did - n't I,   my...

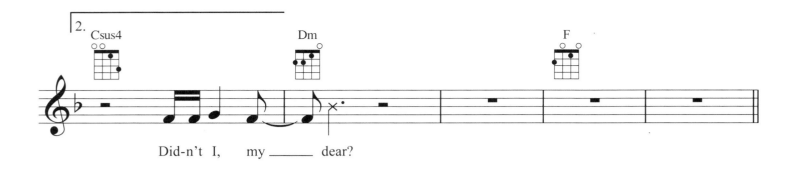

Did-n't I, my _____ dear?

Bridge

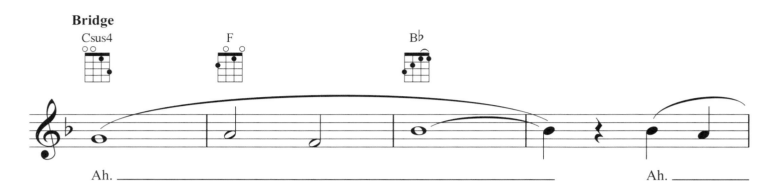

Ah. _____ Ah. _____

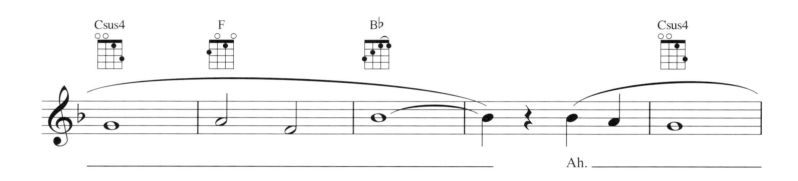

_____ Ah. _____

_____ Ah. _____

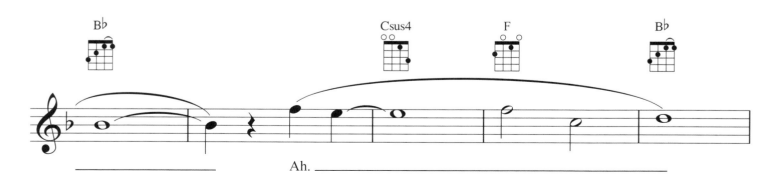

_____ Ah. _____

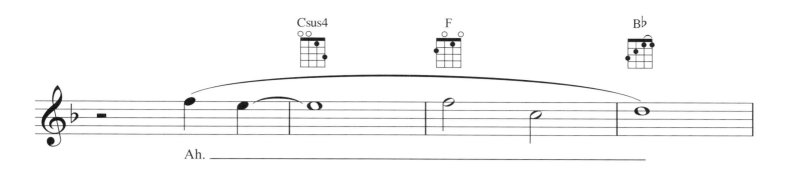

Ah. _____

Outro-Chorus

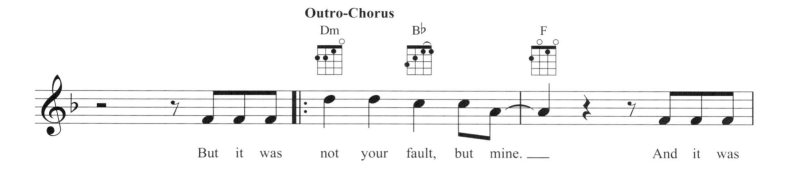

But it was not your fault, but mine. ____ And it was

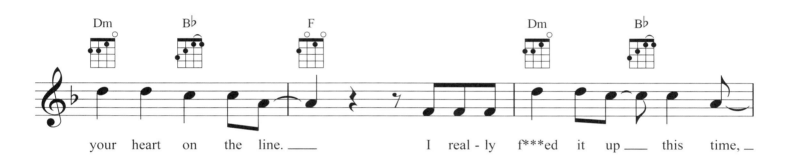

your heart on the line. ____ I real-ly f***ed it up __ this time, __

_____ did - n't I, my _____ dear? _____

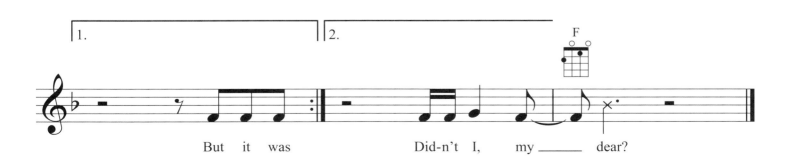

1. But it was   2. Did-n't I, my _____ dear?

Live and Die

Words and Music by Scott Avett, Seth Avett and Robert Crawford

Copyright © 2012 First Big Snow Publishing, Ramseur Family Fold Music, Nemoivmusic and Truth Comes True Publishing
All Rights Administered by BMG Rights Management (US) LLC
All Rights Reserved   Used by Permission

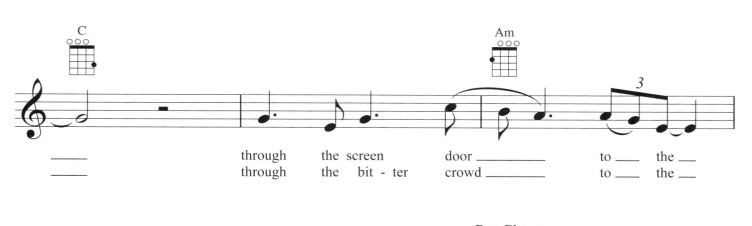

through the screen door _____ to _____ the _____
through the bit - ter crowd _____ to _____ the _____

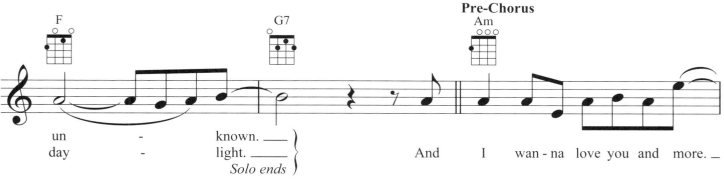

Pre-Chorus

un - known. _____
day - light. _____
Solo ends

And I wan - na love you and more. _____

_____ I wan - na find you and more. _____

Play 1st and 3rd times only

Where do you re - side when you hide? _____ How can I find _____

_____ you? 'Cause I wan - na send you and more. _____

I   wan - na   tempt   you   and   more. _____   Can   you   tell   that

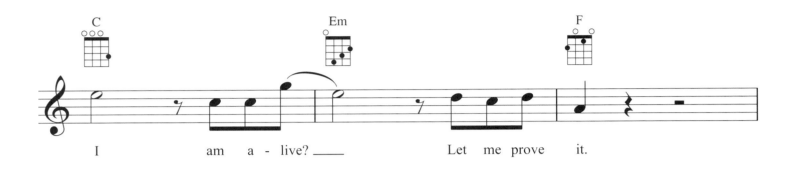

I   am   a - live? ____   Let   me   prove   it.

Chorus

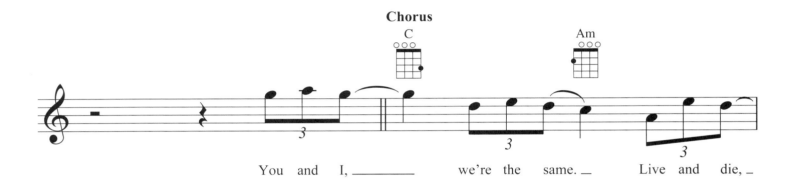

You   and   I, _____   we're   the   same. _   Live   and   die, _

_____   we're   the   same. _ (1.) Hear   my   voice, _____   know   my   name. _   You   and   I, _
                          (2., 3.) You   re - joice, _

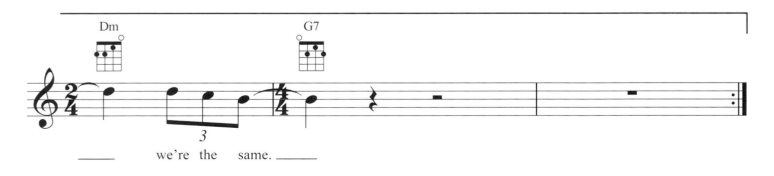

_____   we're   the   same. _____

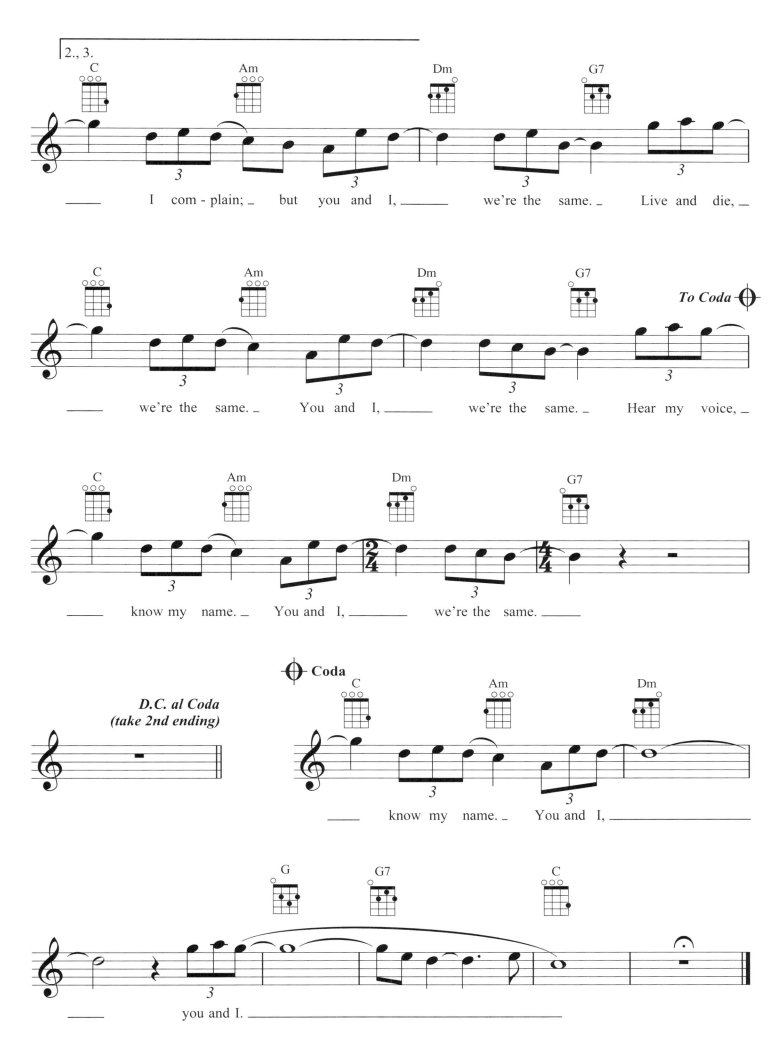

Man on Fire

Words and Music by Alexander Ebert

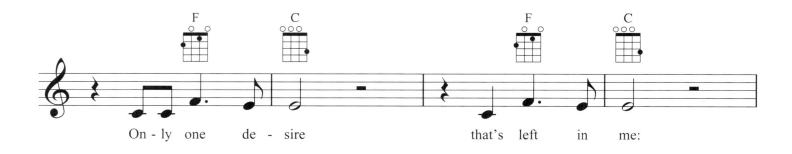

Copyright © 2012 BMG Monarch and Caravan Touchdown
All Rights Administered by BMG Rights Management (US) LLC
All Rights Reserved   Used by Permission

I wan - na know what we've been learn - ing ____ and learn - ing from.

Pre-Chorus

{ Ev - 'ry - bod - y ____ want safe - ty (safe - ty love). _
{ Ev - 'ry - bod - y ____ want ro - mance (ro - mance love). _

____ Ev - 'ry - bod - y ____ want com - fort (com - fort love). _
____ Ev - 'ry - bod - y ____ want safe - ty (safe - ty love). _

____ Ev - 'ry - bod - y ____ want cer - tain (cer - tain love), _
____ Ev - 'ry - bod - y ____ want com - fort (com - fort love), _

____ { ev - 'ry - bod - y ____ but me. ____

Mykonos

Words and Music by Robin Pecknold

Copyright © 2008 Foxes Fellowship
All Rights Administered by Kobalt Songs Music Publishing
All Rights Reserved   Used by Permission

Raging Fire

Words and Music by Phillip Phillips, Gregg Wattenberg, Derek Fuhrmann and Todd Clark

First note

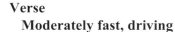

Verse
Moderately fast, driving

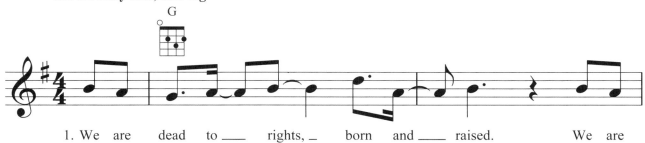

1. We are dead to __ rights, __ born and __ raised. We are

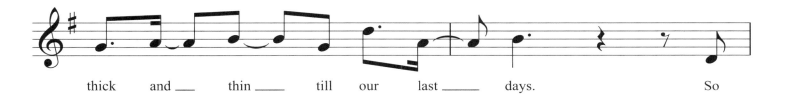

thick and __ thin __ till our last __ days.   So

hold me __ close __ and I'll sur - ren - der __ to your heart.

You know how to __ give __ and how to __ take.   You see

Copyright © 2014 SONGS OF UNIVERSAL, INC., SONGS BY 19 PUBLISHING, PHILPHIL MUSIC, EMI APRIL MUSIC INC.,
G WATT MUSIC, A.E. FUHRMANN PUBLISHING and EGG SONGS PUBLISHING
All Rights for SONGS BY 19 PUBLISHING and PHILPHIL MUSIC Controlled and Administered by SONGS OF UNIVERSAL, INC.
All Rights for EMI APRIL MUSIC INC. and G WATT MUSIC Administered by
SONY/ATV MUSIC PUBLISHING LLC, 424 Church Street, Suite 1200, Nashville, TN 37219
All Rights Reserved   Used by Permission

rag - ing fire, _____

To Coda 2 ⊕

___ in - to a rag - ing fire. Come out, come out, come out; __

_____ won't you turn my soul in - to a rag - ing

To Coda 1 ⊕

fire?   2. You know

Verse

time will __ give __ and time will __ take.   All the

mem - 'ries __ made __ will wash a - way.   E - ven

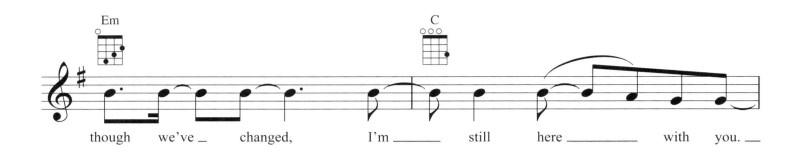

though we've _ changed, I'm _____ still here _____ with you.

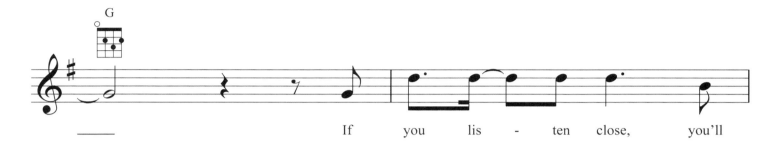

_____ If you lis - ten close, you'll

hear the sound of all _ the ghosts that bring us down. _____

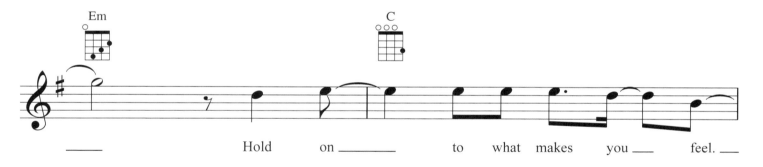

_____ Hold on _____ to what makes you _ feel. _

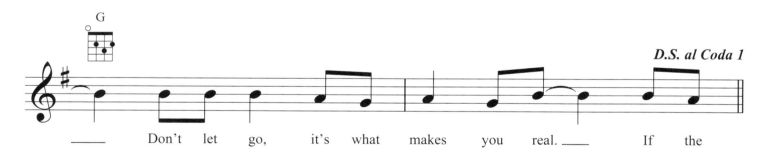

D.S. al Coda 1

_____ Don't let go, it's what makes you real. ___ If the

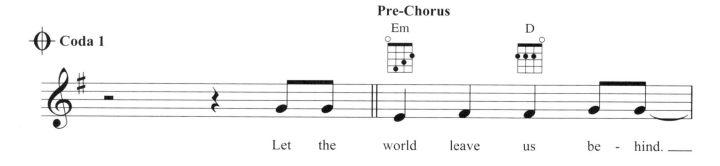

Pre-Chorus

Coda 1

Let the world leave us be - hind. _

The One That Got Away

Words and Music by Joy Williams, John Paul White and Charlie Peacock

1. I never meant to get us in this deep.
2. I got caught up by the chase,

I never meant for this to mean a thing.
and you got high on ev'ry little game.

I wish you were the one,

wish you were the one that got away.

Copyright © 2013 EMI Blackwood Music Inc., Here's To Me Music, Shiny Happy Music and Patron And Profit Publishing
All Rights on behalf of EMI Blackwood Music Inc. and Here's To Me Music Administered by
Sony/ATV Music Publishing LLC, 424 Church Street, Suite 1200, Nashville, TN 37219
All Rights on behalf of Shiny Happy Music Administered by BMG Rights Management (US) LLC
International Copyright Secured   All Rights Reserved

2.

Oh, if I could go ___ back ___ in time, ___

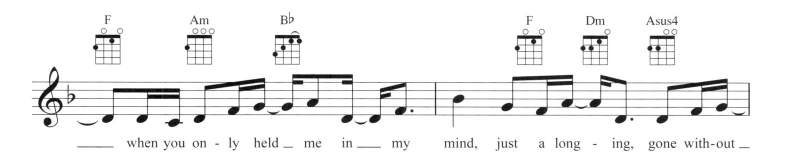

___ when you on - ly held ___ me in ___ my mind, just a long - ing, gone with-out ___

___ a trace. ___ Oh, I wish I'd nev - er

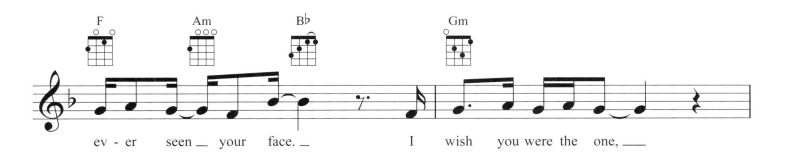

ev - er seen ___ your face. ___ I wish you were the one, ___

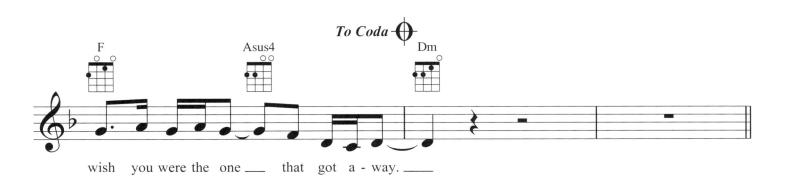

wish you were the one ___ that got a - way. ___

Verse

3. I miss the way you want - ed me _____ when

I was stay - ing just out of _____ your reach, _____

beg - ging for the slight-est touch. _ Ooh, you could-n't get e - nough. _ Mmm. _

D.S. al Coda

Coda

_____ Got a - way _

Bridge

_____ from me, _ got a - way from me _

'fore an - y - bod - y has to bleed. _____

72

Outro-Chorus

73

Poison & Wine

Words and Music by John White, Joy Williams and Chris Lindsey

Copyright © 2009, 2010 EMI Blackwood Music Inc., Mr. Bright Sunshine Publishing, EMI April Music Inc.,
Sensibility Songs, BMG Gold Songs and Little Vampire Music
All Rights on behalf of EMI Blackwood Music Inc., Mr. Bright Sunshine Publishing, EMI April Music Inc. and Sensibility Songs Administered by
Sony/ATV Music Publishing LLC, 424 Church Street, Suite 1200, Nashville, TN 37219
All Rights on behalf of BMG Gold Songs and Little Vampire Music Administered by BMG Rights Management (US) LLC
International Copyright Secured   All Rights Reserved

think your ___ dreams   are the   same   as   mine. ___

Chorus

Male:

Female:
Ooh,   I   don't   love you,   but I   al - ways   will.   Ooh,

I   don't   love you,   but I   al - ways   will.   I   don't   love you,   but I

al - ways   will.   I   al - ways ___ will.   *Female:* 2. I

Verse

wish   you'd   hold   me   when   I   turn   my   back. ___

Male: The   less   I   give,   the more ___ I ___ get   back. ___

75

Chorus

Chorus

Stubborn Love

Words and Music by Jeremy Fraites and Wesley Schultz

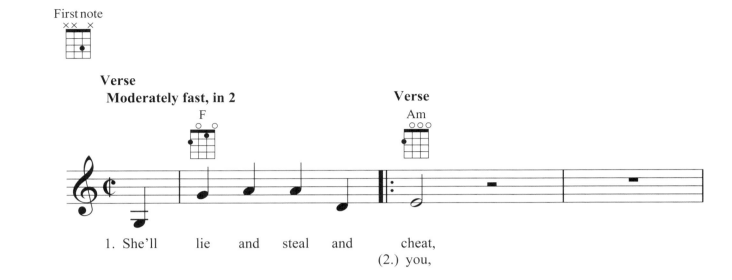

1. She'll lie and steal and cheat,
(2.) you,

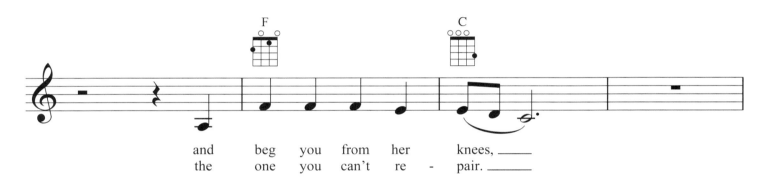

and beg you from her knees, _____
the one you can't re - pair. _____

make you think she means it _____ this time. _____
But I still love her; I don't real - ly care. _____

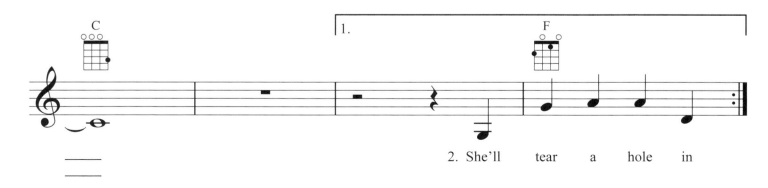

_____
_____
2. She'll tear a hole in

Copyright © 2011 The Lumineers
All Rights Exclusively Administered by Songs Of Kobalt Music Publishing
All Rights Reserved   Used by Permission

noth - ing at all. _____

The op - po - site of love's in - dif -

- fer - ence. _____ So

pay at - ten - tion, now; I'm

stand - ing on your porch scream - ing out, _____

_____ and I won't leave un - til you come _____

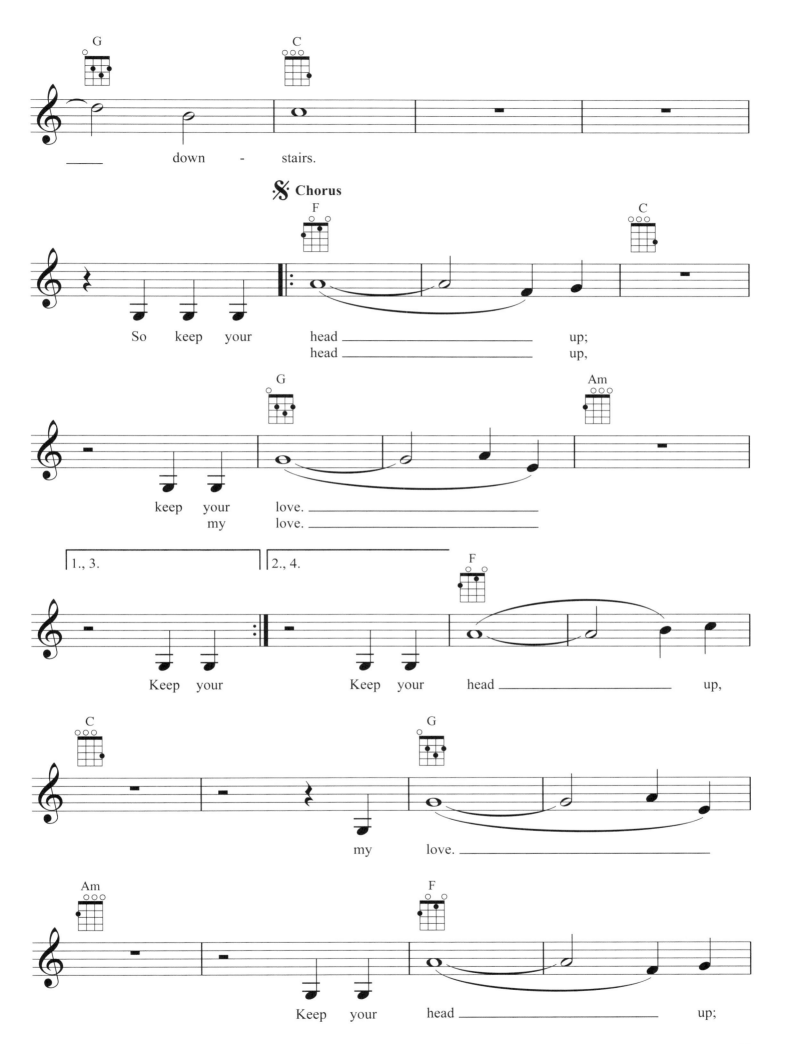

keep your love. _____

To Coda ⊕

4. And I _____ don't blame _ you,

Verse

dear,
(5.) close,

for run - ning like you
but I don't read those

did all _____ these years. _____
things an - y - more. _____

I would do the
I nev - er trust - ed

same, you'd best _____ be - lieve. _____
my _____ own _____ eyes. _____

1.

5. The high - way signs _ say we're

2.

82

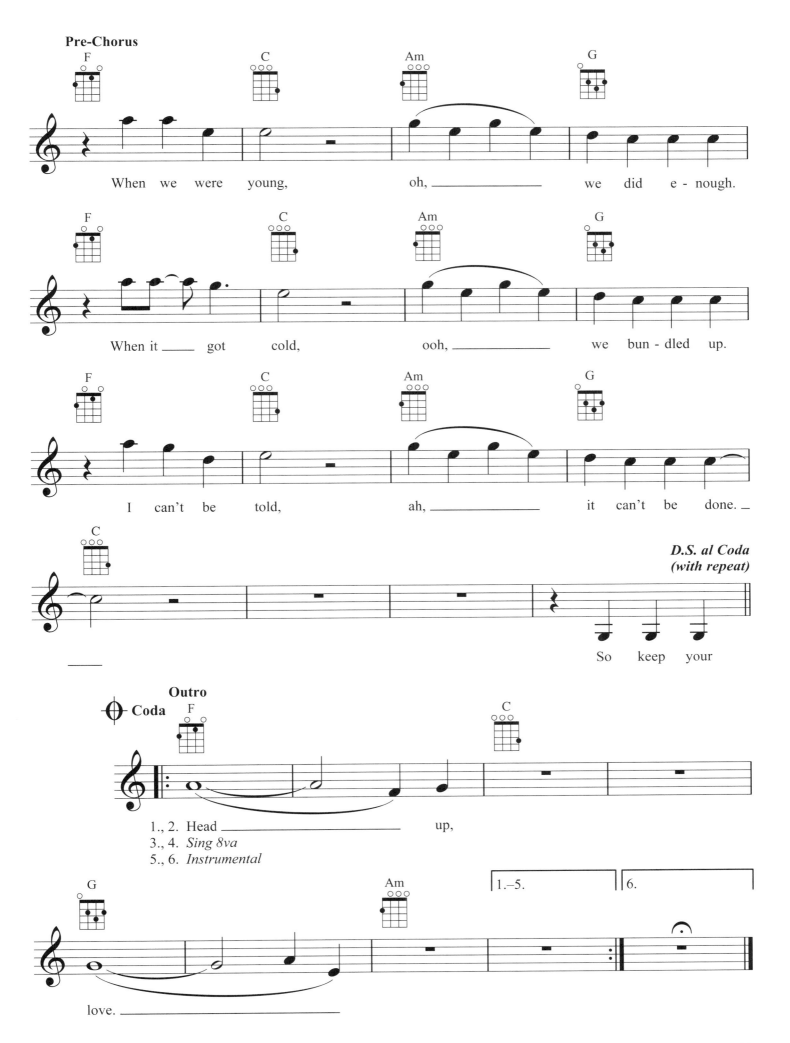

Take 'Em Away

Written by Critter Fuqua

Copyright © 2004 Blood Donor Music
All Rights Administered by Downtown DMP Songs
International Copyright Secured   All Rights Reserved

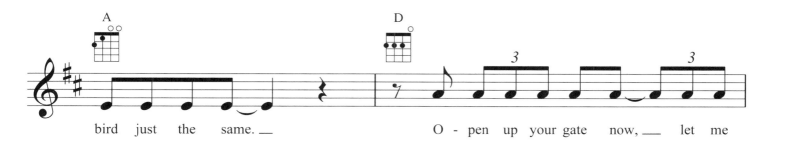

bird just the same. ___   O - pen up your gate now, ___ let me

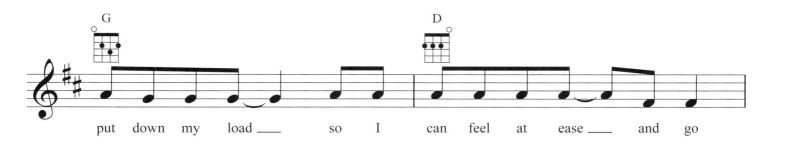

put down my load ___ so I can feel at ease ___ and go

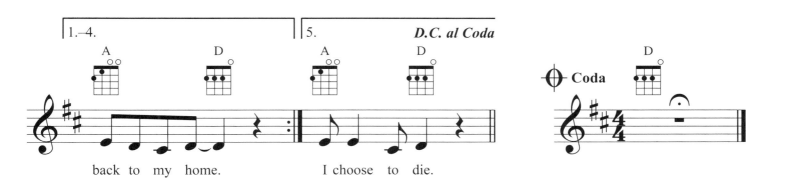

back to my home.   I choose to die.

Additional Lyrics

2. Sun beating down; my legs can't seem to stand.
   There's a boss man at a turnrow with a rifle in his hand.
   I got nine children, nothing in the pan.
   My wife, she died hungry while I was plowing land.

3. Can't see when I go to work, can't see when I get off.
   How do you expect a man not to get lost?
   Every year I just keep getting deeper in debt.
   If there's a happy day, Lord, I haven't seen one yet.

4. Land that I love is the land that I'm working,
   But it's hard to love it all the time when your back is a-hurting.
   Getting too old now to push this here plow.
   Please let me lay down so I can look at the clouds.

5. Land that I know is where two rivers collide:
   The Brazos and the Navaso' and the big blue sky.
   Flood plains, freight trains, watermelon vines;
   Of any place on God's green earth, this is where I choose to die.

Skinny Love

Words and Music by Justin Vernon

Copyright © 2008 April Base Publishing and Chris In The Morning Music LLC
All Rights Administered Worldwide by Kobalt Songs Music Publishing
All Rights Reserved   Used by Permission

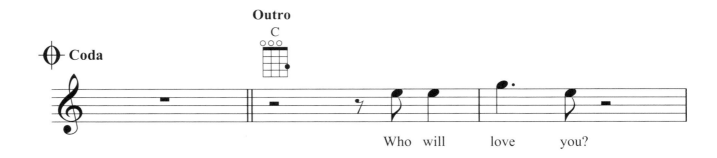

Who will love you?

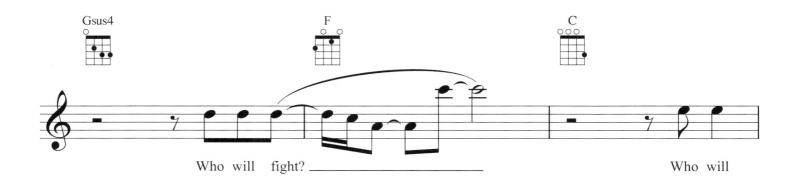

Who will fight? _____ Who will

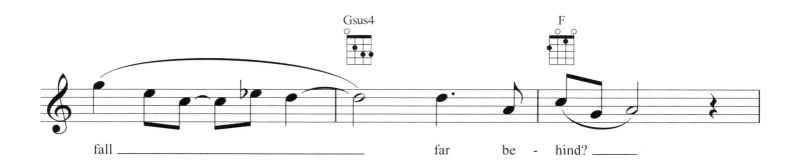

fall _____ far be - hind? _____

Ooh. _____

Additional Lyrics

2. I tell my love to wreck it all,
   Cut out all the ropes and let me fall.
   My my my, my my my, my my.
   Right in this moment, this order's tall.

3. Come on, skinny love, what happened here?
   We suckle on the hope in light brassieres.
   My my my, my my my, my my.
   Sullen load is full, so slow on the split.